MW00593217

RAILS
ACROSS
AMERICA

BY RENA KORB

Editorial Offices: Glenview, Illinois • Parsippany, New Jersey • New York, New York

Sales Offices: Needham, Massachusetts • Duluth, Georgia • Glenview, Illinois
Coppell, Texas • Sacramento, California • Mesa, Arizona

Moving West

In May 1869 the nation's first **transcontinental railroad** was finished. The railroad stretched from coast to coast. Now people could travel across the country in ten days or less.

Before 1869 people had only a few ways to travel west. Some sailed around the tip of South America or to Panama and back up along the Pacific coast. Others rode across the country in covered wagons. Those methods of **transportation** took many months.

Travel Today

Today people have many choices when they travel across the country. Many choose to fly because it is the fastest way. Others drive their cars, take a bus, or go by train.

Railroad owners were sure that trains would replace horses.

The Transcontinental Railroad

A transcontinental railroad was first suggested in 1832. However, many people thought the idea was impossible. At that time the longest railroad track was only 136 miles long.

During the 1800s many people believed that the United States would expand to the Pacific Ocean. In 1848 the country gained land in the Southwest after winning a war against Mexico. California became a state in 1850.

In 1853 the United States government sent **engineers** to study possible routes for a transcontinental railroad. While Congress argued about which route was best, a railroad engineer named Theodore Judah took action.

In 1861 Judah convinced four California businesspeople to form the Central Pacific Railroad Company. They became known as the "Big Four."

Leland Stanford was one of the "Big Four." He was a state governor.

Engine Operated Over Central Pacific R.R. Out of Sacramento, Cal.

This postcard shows the first engine to run on the Central Pacific Railroad from Sacramento, California.

In 1862 Congress passed the Pacific Railway Act. It gave the Central Pacific the right to lay tracks going eastward. The government also created the Union Pacific Railroad Company to lay tracks going westward. The two lines would meet somewhere in the middle.

Building the Railroad

In January 1863, Central Pacific officials and workers met in Sacramento, California. Many steps went into building the railroad. Engineers chose the best path. Workers cleared away trees and stones. They placed crossties, or wooden beams that connect and support the rails of a railroad, into the ground. They then hammered iron rails onto the crossties with spikes.

On the Central Pacific Railroad

The Central Pacific had hundreds of miles of track to lay, but not enough workers. The work was hard and dangerous. By early 1865 only a few hundred Irish **immigrants** had jobs as the railroad crew.

The Central Pacific solved its problem by hiring Chinese immigrants. By the time the railroad was finished, about ten thousand Chinese immigrants had done most of the work.

Many workers on the transcontinental railroad were Chinese immigrants.

During the winter of 1866–1867, snowslides killed dozens of workers.

Crossing the Sierra Nevada

The Central Pacific crews faced the hardest part of their job after they left Sacramento. They had to lay tracks across the Sierra Nevada.

Crews worked six days a week. They blew up cliffs and dug tunnels through rock. Crews used picks, shovels, axes, animals, wheelbarrows, and gunpowder to do the job.

The winter of 1866–1867 was harsh. There were freezing temperatures, piles of snow, and dozens of storms. The men lived in tunnels underneath the snow or in shacks on the mountain. That winter the track moved forward only about eight inches a day.

Work on the Union Pacific

By the end of 1863, the Union Pacific rail line reached as far west as Omaha, Nebraska. The Civil War delayed more work until 1865.

Workers on the Union Pacific faced problems from American Indians, or Native Americans, who lived in the region. The railroad tracks ran through buffalo hunting grounds, causing the American Indians to attack the railroad crews.

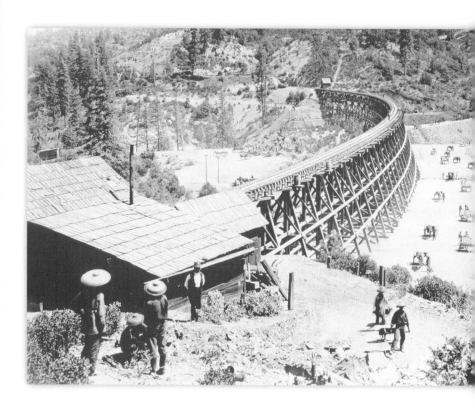

The Race to Utah

By 1868 the Central Pacific rail line extended eastward from the Sierra Nevada. The rail lines made by both companies were now on flat land. Workers on both sides rushed to complete the most track.

In 1869 both companies were working on tracks that did not connect. The government forced officials from the two companies to meet. The officials picked a spot where the railroad tracks would join: Promontory, Utah.

Sometimes long wooden structures called trestles were built to carry the rail line across valleys.

The two railroad crews now raced to be first to reach Promontory Summit. One day, workers from the Central Pacific laid six miles of track. Soon after, the Union Pacific crews laid seven miles of track in one day.

On April 28, 1869, a Central Pacific crew worked from sunrise until seven o'clock at night. It set a record by completing more than ten miles of track in one day.

On April 30 the Central Pacific workers reached Promontory and won the race to the end. The next day the Union Pacific crews came within sight of Promontory. The transcontinental railroad was almost done. In six years workers had built 1,780 miles of track.

The First Transcontinental Railroad, 1869

Done!

The railroad companies planned a big celebration in Utah. On May 10, 1869, only one more spike was needed to connect the two rail lines. Workers, officials, reporters, and guests gathered at the site.

A crew member drove in the last spike. It was made of solid gold. The news went out: "Done!" People around the country joined in the celebration. They made speeches, held parades, and rang bells.

The completion of the transcontinental railroad opened up travel to the West.

Early train travel offered a new level of speed and comfort for travelers.

Traveling Out West

People from all over the country wanted to ride along the new route. Each week, one train headed west and another headed east.

The transcontinental railroad opened up the United States to tourists, travel reporters, and people looking for jobs. Soon even more railroads connected communities from coast to coast.

Glossary

engineer a person who uses scientific and mathematical ideas to design, make, and run structures and machines

immigrant a person who comes to live in a new land

transcontinental railroad a railroad that crosses a continent

transportation the moving of goods, people, or animals from one place to another